Time Is When

Beth Gleick

Illustrated by Marthe Jocelyn

Tundra Books

Published in Canada by Tundra Books,
75 Sherbourne Street, Toronto, Ontario M5A 2P9

Published in the United States by Tundra Books of Northern New York,
P.O. Box 1030, Plattsburgh, New York 12901

Library of Congress Control Number: 2007938540

Library and Archives Canada Cataloguing in Publication

Gleick, Beth
    Time is when / Beth Gleick ; illustrations by Marthe Jocelyn.

Target audience: For ages 3–6.
ISBN 978-0-88776-870-5

    1. Time – Juvenile literature.   I. Jocelyn, Marthe   II. Title.
QB209.5.G54 2008   j529'.7   C2007-906102-8

We acknowledge the financial support of the Government of Canada through the Book Publishing Industry Development Program (BPIDP) and that of the Government of Ontario through the Ontario Media Development Corporation's Ontario Book Initiative.

We further acknowledge the support of the Canada Council for the Arts and the Ontario Arts Council for our publishing program.

ONTARIO ARTS COUNCIL
CONSEIL DES ARTS DE L'ONTARIO

Medium: Fabric and paper collage

Printed in China

1 2 3 4 5 6   13 12 11 10 09 08

For Daniel, Harry, Jeremy, Maggie, and Julia – *B.G.*

For Jim and Cynthia – *M.J.*

Time is
from before to now;
from now to later.

Time is seconds, minutes, hours,
days, weeks, months, and years.

Time ticks by on clocks and watches.

Time moves on through
pages on calendars.

Time is when.

In one second, you can
bounce a ball, or jump,

or say hello,

or turn a page.

A minute has 60 seconds.

In one minute, you can
walk one block

(if you walk quickly and
don't stop to look in the
store windows).

An hour has 60 minutes.

In one hour, you can paint a picture
or build a make-believe city.

A day has 24 hours. It starts at midnight,
while you are sleeping. It has a morning,
a noon, an afternoon, and an evening.
And then it ends at midnight,
again while you are sleeping.

In one day, you can do many things.
Sometimes you do the same things
every day; sometimes you do
different things.

In a morning, you can
get up out of bed,

eat breakfast,

and go to school.

At noon, you can eat lunch.
In an afternoon, you can swing
and climb and ride.

In an evening, you can eat
supper and read a book,
or watch television.

At night,
you sleep.

While you are sleeping,
a new day begins.

There are seven days in a week.

From Sunday until the next
Sunday is one week.

April

Sunday	Monday	Tuesday	Wednesday	Thursday	Friday	Saturday
		1	2	3	4	5
6	7	8	9	10	11	12
13	14	15	16	17	18	19
20	21	22	23	24	25	26
27	28	29	30			

There are about four weeks in one
month and 52 weeks in one year.

A year has 12 months
and four seasons.

From January until the next
January is one year.

In some parts of the world, the start of the New Year is winter – trees without leaves, cold weather, and snow.

The spring months are often windy,
warm, and rainy. The grass turns green,
trees sprout leaves, flowers bloom,
and birds sing.

In many places, the summer months
have bright sunshine and crashing
thunderstorms. Summer is usually
a good time for boating,
swimming, and fishing.

The fall months have cooler weather.
The leaves turn red, yellow, and brown,
and the wind blows them off the trees.
It is the end of another year.

From your last birthday to your next
birthday is one year.

In the many seconds, minutes, hours, days,
weeks, and months that make up one year,
you can do many things.

But most important of all, you grow one year older.

The time past is yesterday, and all of the days, weeks, months, and years that are behind you.

The time now, the present time, is today – this hour, this minute, this second.

The future time is tomorrow, and
all of the days, weeks, months,
and years that are ahead of you.

Time is from before to now;
from now to later.

Time is when.